The Essence of Re

Usui Reiki Level 2 Advanced Practitioner Manual

A Complete Guide to the Usui Method of Natural Healing

by

Adele and Garry Malone

Reiki Masters/Teachers Since 1997

www.reiki-store.co.uk | www.reiki-store.com

© Copyright Notice

The Essence of Reiki 2
Usui Reiki Level 2 Advanced Practitioner Manual

Published by
GarryMalone.com Limited.
www.reiki-store.co.uk
www.reiki-store.com

Our Reiki Line Lineage

Dr Mikao Usui

Dr Chujiro Hayashi

Madam Hawayo Takata

Iris Ishikura

Arthur Robertson

Rick & Emma Ferguson

Margarette L Shelton

Kathleen Ann Milner

Robert N Wachsberger

Tricia Courtney-Dickens

Adele and Garry Malone

About the Authors

Adele and Garry Malone are highly experienced **Certified** Reiki Masters/Teachers, Life Coaches, Clinical Hypnotherapists and Master Practitioners of NLP who run a successful and busy practice from their Home Office and Healing Centre in Hertfordshire UK.

Since 1997 their combined practical Reiki experience and professional easy to follow books, workshops and home study courses, have offered the Reiki reader/student an holistic approach to the study, mastery and use of the USUI method of natural healing.

Adele and Garry have jointly authored a number of best-selling books, audio and visual programmes, certified home study courses and conduct Reiki and Personal Development workshops throughout the UK and Internationally.

Authors & Publishers Disclaimer

Reiki is an ancient form of healing that is practised by the authors and numerous practitioners around the world. The information and techniques in this book do not constitute medical advice. Healing and medicine are two very different disciplines. You should always remember to seek medical advice from a qualified doctor or practitioner in the case of serious illness. While all suggested treatments are offered in good faith, the author and publisher cannot accept responsibility for any illness arising out of the failure by the reader/individual to seek medical advice from a qualified doctor or medical practitioner.

Special Acknowledgement

Adele and Garry Malone would like to thank their Reiki Lineage especially Reiki Master **Tricia Courtney-Dickens**, for her wonderful ability to teach Reiki with such clarity and for passing on to them both this special gift of healing.

The Essence of Reiki 2 is **dedicated to our four wonderful children** Molly, Harriette-Rose, Charlotte and Garry.

In Memory
of
Kim Buckley

Important Note to the Reader

The purpose of this book is to give the reader a comprehensive guide to the teachings and disciplines associated with Second Degree Usui Reiki. We have purposely kept the information concise so the reader can quickly and easily understand and apply Reiki.

Wherever possible we have avoided adding personal beliefs that may differ from the traditional teachings of Dr Mikao Usui. The knowledge and information contained in this book is based on the original **Shiki Ryoho** Method of Healing developed by **Dr Usui** over two hundred years ago.

If you desire to use the teachings contain within this book to heal yourself and others you must first have received the necessary attunements from a Reiki Master either in person or via distant attunement. You can find out how to become a Certified Usui Reiki Master Teacher with our Best Selling Reiki Master Video Home Study Course by visiting www.reiki-store.co.uk

If thou canst believe, all things are possible
to him that believeth. – Mark 9:23

Table of Contents

1

An Introduction to 2nd Degree Usui Reiki

"It is a denial of the divinity within us to doubt our potential and our possibilities." — James E. Faust

Reiki 2 - A New Beginning with New Possibilities

A Moment of Reflection

First degree Reiki is the beginning of an exciting and profound journey filled with self discovery, personal change, love, growth, new experiences and an immeasurable sense of bonding with a higher power.

It takes most people from a position of scepticism and propels them into a new understanding of life.

Reiki opens up doors to new dimensions, to things we never dreamt possible, and gives us access to the purest unconditional love available.

Reiki is pure energy; it is omnipresent, omnipotent and omniscient. Reiki is available to all who wish to tap into it, accept it, and become one with its energy and wisdom.

Words cannot adequately describe Reiki, it needs to be experienced. Every person experiences Reiki in different ways, which is why it is impossible to define Reiki clearly in words. Whether you experience Reiki as a treatment from a Reiki practitioner or by attending a workshop, it will change your life for the better if you are open to the energy and allow it to envelop your mind, body and spirit.

THE SECOND DEGREE

The second degree is the next giant step towards understanding and becoming fully attuned to Reiki.

Everyone who wants to study and master the second degree must first have already completed the first degree either in a workshop or a home study course. Reiki 1 is of course included within our Reiki Master Home Study Course.

Students need to have been given the first degree attunements and the knowledge required to skilfully work with Reiki. Unlike the first degree, students normally would have obtained experience, skill and a level of intuitive understanding towards the unlimited power of Reiki.

Most second degree students no longer fear or harbour scepticism towards Reiki. They are normally enthusiastic and excited about the prospect of enhancing their skills and understanding. It is often recommended that the student/practitioner takes time after the first degree workshop to assimilate; and incorporate the teachings of Dr. Usui into their practice and daily life, before attending a second degree workshop. Make sure you are attending the second degree workshop for the right reasons.

Like the first degree, most people feel they are drawn at the appropriate time to the next level of Reiki. Often an event or strong feeling can direct you towards this new path. The main criteria for attending the reiki 2 workshop is; that you personally feel ready to go forward with Reiki.

Trying To Understand How the Second Degree Works

It is almost impossible to explain how second degree Reiki actually works in a way that everyone can understand and accept it. To try to scientifically and logically grasp how the universal life force functions is beyond human intelligence. Like so many things in life, although we do not fully understand how they work we still use them to improve our lives.

Many people would find it extremely difficult to explain how electricity, televisions, faxes, computers, telephones and microwaves or the internet works for example. However, not being able to comprehend how they work doesn't stop people using them. Likewise, although no-one can completely explain how Reiki works it shouldn't stop you using and trusting in its ability to improve your life and the lives of the people you work with.

When you study, experience and work with the teachings and techniques of the second degree you will be able to make your own judgement on how you feel it works. Alternatively you could simply do what we recommend and just believe in its infinitive wisdom and let go of any doubts and fears.

However, for those who wish a brief insight into the second degree we will attempt to justly explain our own understanding of how the second degree works.

How We Believe Reiki Works

Reiki is omnipresent-present everywhere at the same time.

Reiki is omnipotent-absolute and infinite power.

Reiki is omniscient-infinite wisdom and knowledge.

The universal life force connects all living things together like a vast ocean. As droplets in this ocean we are communicating with and are connected to, all other droplets in this ocean on an unconscious level. Similarly, every cell in the human body has its own individual position and responsibility. However, each cell is also unequivocally connected to and is unconsciously communicating with all the other fifty-trillion cells in the body. Deepak Chopra, in his book Quantum Healing also talks about how the entire universe is connected.

He explains how particles that are separated by immense distances of time and space know what one another are doing. When an electron for example jumps into a new orbit on the outside of an atom, the anti-electron (positron) paired with it must also react no matter where it lives in the universe. Each particle in our universe has an intelligence that communicates across time and space.

Scientists studying the behaviour of monkeys on the coast of Japan noticed one day a particular monkey had begun dipping his sweet potatoes into salt water before eating them. Shortly afterwards they found all the monkeys within the colony were also dipping their potatoes into salt water.

The scientist assumed the monkeys were just copying each other until they discovered monkeys in other parts of the world had begun dipping their potatoes into salt water also. The monkeys were communicating through an unknown intelligence across time and space. The scientists labelled this intelligent communication Morphic Resonance.

Interestingly another study found when giraffes began causing serious damage to trees by eating more of the tree than normal, the trees responded by increasing the amount of tannin in their leaves. This defensive action made the leaves too bitter for the giraffes to eat. Scientists discovered the trees were communicating with gases — an energy with intelligence. Likewise, Reiki is also energy with intelligence.

No man was ever wise by chance. -Seneca

2

Gassho the First Pillar of Reiki

"We know what we are, but not what we may be." — *William Shakespeare*

The five Reiki principles which are taught in Reiki Level 1 are based on the three pillars of Reiki:

Gassho: Pronounced – Gash-Show

Reiji-Ho: Pronounced - Ray-Gee-Hoe

Chiryo: Pronounced – Chi-Rye-Oh

In this lesson we are going to discuss the First Pillar of Reiki – Gassho.

Gassho – Placing the Two Palms Together

Gassho literally means "two hands coming together." It is a ritual gesture formed by placing the hands – palms together, in the 'prayer' or 'praying hands' position as illustrated above; and is the most fundamental and also the most frequently used of all the hand gestures (also known as (in-zou) and (mudras)) in the practice of Buddhism.

Gassho implies recognition of the oneness of all beings and is used to:

Express Gratitude and Respect

For focus; to prevent wandering of the mind

To bring oneself into dynamic balance

To express the One Mind – totality: congruence of being.

There are actually two primary forms of the traditional gassho: They are known as:

Formal Gassho

This is used in formal situations such as rituals and religious services. The hands are brought together in front of the face, fingers straight pointing up, palms pressing together. Elbows are raised, forearms at about 30° angles to the floor; fingertips at about the same level as the top of the nose, but hands roughly a fist's distance in front of the tip of the nose. The eyes are focused on the tips of the middle fingers.

The formal Gassho helps establish a reverential, alert attitude. This gesture is used to show reverence.

Mu-shin ('No-Mind') Gassho

This form of gassho used primarily in greetings. Here, the hands are held loosely together – the tips of the fingers/thumbs still touch, yet there is a slight space between the palms. The forearms are at about 45° angles to the floor. The hands are still held at the equivalent of approximately one fist's distance in front of the tip of the nose, but the hands are lower, in front of the mouth – the fingertips at a level just below the nose.

The eyes are focused on the tips of the middle fingers. Many people also perform mu-shin gassho with hands positioned in front of the chest at a level just above the heart.

Beyond the 'Standard/Primary' Gassho, there are a number of other special versions of this found in Buddhism.

For example:

The Lotus Gassho – this is almost identical to mu-shin gassho, however the fingers are bent slightly more and the tips of the middle fingers are held about an inch apart. The Lotus Gassho is primarily used by priests during particular ceremonies or rites.

The Diamond Gassho – also called the 'gassho of oneness with all life' – this is almost identical to mu-shin gassho, however the fingers are perfectly straight and interlocked. As with the Lotus Gassho, the Diamond Gassho is primarily used by priests during particular ceremonies or rites.

Dr Usui Taught His Students the Gassho Meditation

Dr. Mikao Usui taught a meditation called the Gassho Meditation. This meditation was practiced at the beginning of every Reiki workshop and meeting.

Usui, instructed his students to practice the meditation each morning and evening for 5-20 minutes. Gassho is so simple, that anyone can practice it alone or in a group meditation.

We recommend you try it; then only if you enjoy it and find it beneficial, commit to practicing it every day for at least thirty days. During this time you could also keep a Meditation Journal to record your experiences with Gassho, and details of any benefits you have noticed over the course of the month. Many find the Gassho Meditation brings more focus and clarity into their lives and enables them to become more relax, centred and more productive and creative during in their daily life.

The Gassho Meditation

(Take Time out 5-20 Minutes a Day)

Sit down, close your eyes and place hands together in front of your chest (prayer position).

Focus your attention at the point where the two middle fingers meet.

Let go of everything else. If your mind wanders, acknowledge the thought, let it go and just refocus returning to the point where your middle fingers meet.

Repeat the five reiki principles either aloud or internally.

If you find it uncomfortable to hold your hands in Gassho for 5-20 minutes, simply let your hands (kept together) slowly drop down onto your lap finding a more comfortable position to continue the meditation.

You may observe energy in the form of heat, cold or images, just let it go and return your focal point to the tips of your two middle fingers.

If you need to adjust your posture; move slowly, deliberately and consciously. It is easier and better to meditate with a straight spinal column, keeping your head still.

If you suffer from back problems or find it difficult to sit still; try sitting on a straight back chair with a few pillows for comfort.

Alternatively, you can sit on the floor on a few cushions with your back against a wall. You could even meditate while lying down or a sofa or bed, but you may find you fall asleep, which at night is OK, but in the morning could leave you late for work or other engagements.

What is healing, but a shift in perspectives? ~ Mark Doty

3

Reiji-Ho the Second Pillar of Reiki

"I have a habit of letting my imagination run away from me. It always comes back though . . . drenched with possibilities." — Valaida Fullwood

Translated into English, Reiji means "indication of the Reiki power." Ho means "methods." Reiji-Ho consists of three short rituals that are carried out before each treatment:

Fold your hands in front of your chest in the Gassho position with your eyes closed. Now connect with the Reiki power. This is very simple: Ask the Reiki power to flow through you. Within a few seconds, you will become aware of the Reiki energy flow. It may enter through your crown chakra or you experience it in your hands or heart chakra. Second Degree practitioners or Reiki masters can use the distance healing symbol to connect with the Reiki power. Repeat the wish three times in your mind that Reiki may flow, then send the mental-healing symbol and seal it all with the power symbol. As soon as you feel the energy, continue on to the next step.

Pray for the recovery and/or health of the patient on all levels, let Reiki do what is required. Raise your hands up (still in Gassho) in front of your third eye and ask the Reiki power to guide your hands to where the energy is needed.

Then use and follow your intuition. This technique guides your hands like magnets to the places on the body that needs treatment. Trusting your intuition when you first practice Reiki can be either easy or difficult. Trust in the phenomenon that is Reiki. Totally detach yourself from seeking after possible outcomes; just let go and believe in Reiki. Invite and allow Reiki to 'call' (i.e. guide / draw your hands automatically – spontaneously) to any areas of the recipients body that may be in need of treatment. Allow your hands to move where they are drawn – let go – trust – resist the urge to 'do'. When it comes to letting Reiki guide you, different people may receive their guidance in different ways. Some may simply experience pure spontaneous movement – as if being 'pulled' magnetically; some may experience images in the mind's-eye of where treatment is needed; others may 'hear' where Reiki is needed, and so on. If nothing seems to happen – if you are not aware of 'receiving guidance' (and when first performing Reiki it isn't always necessarily that obvious) recall the precepts: '...'don't worry...' It will come in time – and when it does, you will know. Reiki will guide you. Reiki will flow – and as usual, the flow will taper off when the area has taken sufficient treatment – and then your hands will be 'called' to the next area.

When there are no more areas requiring treatment (or, as is sometimes the case, there are no areas at all requiring treatment) your hands will be guided to rest, palms down, on your thighs / in your lap. Conclude Reiji Ho by once more performing gassho.

REIJI-HO

Step 1:
Hands in Gassho;
Connect to Reiki

Step 2:
Pray for the Recipients Health & Well Being. Raise Hands to Third Eye ask the Reiki power to guide your hands to where the energy is needed.

Step 3:
Use Your Intuition

Healing is simply attempting to do more of those things that bring Joy and fewer of those things that bring pain. ~ O. Carl Simonton

4

Chiryo the Third Pillar of Reiki

*"Just because a path never existed,
doesn't mean that it isn't there..."* — *Lionel Suggs*

Chiryo means "treatment" in English.

The person giving the treatment holds their dominant hand above the client's crown chakra (see photo) and waits until there is an impulse or inspiration, which the hand then follows.

During the treatment the reiki practitioner uses their intuition; giving free rein to their hands, sensing painful areas of the body to work on and moving from those areas only when they no longer hurt or until the hands lift from the body on their own and move onto a new area to treat.

The Breath

The bridge between the body and consciousness is the breath. In all esoteric traditions, there is knowledge of the special meaning of the breath. Just as we breathe in oxygen for basic survival, we also inhale the universal life force which nourishes and cleanses our mind body and spirit.

Dr Usui taught a breathing technique called Joshin Kokyuu-Ho which means breathing to cleanse the spirit.

Joshin Kokyuu-Ho

Begin by sitting down comfortably and relaxing your body, keeping your spine as straight as possible.

Inhale slowly through your nose. Imagine that as well as breathing in air through your nose, you are also drawing Reiki energy through your crown chakra.

Become aware of how you experience Reiki being drawn through the crown chakra, while you continue to breathe calmly and serenely.

Over time with practice, the positive effect of this exercise and a strong feel of the energy flowing through you will become more apparent.

During this breathing exercise you will feel your entire body being invigorated and enriched with Reiki energy. Draw your breath deep down into your belly, down to the energy centre just below the navel. In Japan, this centre is called Tanden, and the Chinese call it Tantien.

The Tanden (Tantien)

The Tanden is the centre of the body, the seat of a person's vitality.

Hold your breath and the energy you have drawn in with it in the Tanden for a few seconds.

Your aim is to supply the body with love and energy. Be gentle.

While holding your breath, imagine that the energy from the Tanden spreads throughout your entire body and energising and invigorating it.

Now exhale through your mouth. While doing this, imagine that the breath and the Reiki energy not only flow out of your mouth, but also from your fingertips and the tips of your toes and out of your hand and foot chakras.

This is how we become a clear channel of Reiki. The energy flows into us from the cosmos and back again to the cosmos. The energy cycle from the macrocosm to the microcosm, and vice versa, has been completed.

In Tai Chi and Qigong, the following is always recommended for similar breathing exercises: Keep the tongue on the roof of your mouth, touching your front teeth while inhaling and then let it come down and rest on the bottom of the mouth while exhaling.

Experiment with this technique while you treat yourself or others.

A painful time in our life is what I call a "healing crisis." We are letting go of something old and opening to something new. ~ Shakti Gawain

5

Namaste

"Knowing yourself is the beginning of all wisdom." — Aristotle

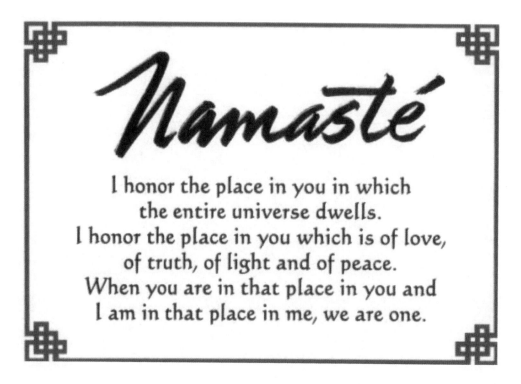

Namasté

I honor the place in you in which
the entire universe dwells.
I honor the place in you which is of love,
of truth, of light and of peace.
When you are in that place in you and
I am in that place in me, we are one.

The gesture (or mudra) of Namaste is a simple act made by bringing together both palms of the hands before the heart, and lightly bowing the head. In the simplest of terms it is accepted as a humble greeting straight from the heart and reciprocated accordingly.

Namaste is pronounced "Namastay", and is a composite of two Sanskrit words, Nama, and te. Te means you, and Nama means to bend, incline or bow. The meaning of these two words together is a sense of submitting oneself to another, with complete humility.

The word nama is split into two, na and ma. Na signifies negation and ma represents mine. The meaning would then be 'not mine'. The import being that the individual soul belongs entirely to the Supreme soul, which is identified as residing in the individual towards whom the Namaste is directed. Indeed there is nothing that the soul can claim as its own. Namaste is thus the necessary rejection of 'I' and the associated phenomena of egotism. It is said that 'ma' in nama means death (spiritual), and when this is negated (na-ma), it signifies immortality.

The whole action of Namaste unfolds itself at three levels:

Mental

Physical

Verbal

The mental submission is in the spirit of total surrender of the self. This is parallel to the devotion one expresses before a chosen deity, also known as bhakti. The devotee who thus venerates with complete self-surrender is believed to partake the merits or qualities of the person or deity before whom he performs this submission. A transaction can only be between equals, between individuals who share some details in common. Hence by performing Namaste before an individual we recognise the divine spark in him. Further by facilitating our partaking of these divine qualities, Namaste makes us aware of these very characteristics residing within our own selves. Simply put, Namaste intimates the following:

The God in me greets the God in you.

The Spirit in me meets the same Spirit in you.

In other words, it recognizes the equality of all, and pays honour to the sacredness of all and everyone, regardless of age, status or wealth. Translated into a bodily act, Namaste is deeply rich in symbolism. Firstly the proper performance of Namaste requires that we blend the five fingers of the left hand exactly with the fingers of the right hand. The significance behind this simple act in fact governs the entire gamut of our active life. The five fingers of the left hand represent the five senses of karma and those of the right hand the five organs of knowledge. Hence it signifies that our karma or action must be in harmony, and governed by rightful knowledge, prompting us to think and act correctly.

Namaste recognizes the duality that has forever existed in this world and suggests an effort on our part to bring these two forces together, ultimately leading to a higher unity and non-dual state of Oneness. Some of these dual elements which the gesture of Namaste marries together and unifies as one include:

God and Goddess

Man and Woman

Heaven and Earth

Sun and Moon

Theory and Practice

Wisdom and Method

Pleasure and Pain

Astral body (consciousness) and Etheric body (sensation)

Mind and body

Conscious and Unconscious

Intellect and Instinct

Reason and Emotion

Thought and Feeling

Word and Meaning

Finally, the gesture of Namaste is unique also in the sense that its physical performance is accompanied by a verbal utterance of the word "Namaste." This practice is equivalent to the chanting of a mantra. The sonority of the sacred sound 'Namaste' is believed to have a quasi-magical value, corresponding to a creative energy change. This transformation is that of aligning oneself in harmony with the vibration of the cosmos itself. At its most general Namaste is a social transaction. It is usual for individuals to greet when they meet each other. It is not only a sign of recognition but also an expression of happiness at each other's sight. This initial conviviality sets the positive tone for the further development of a harmonious relationship.

Namaste as a greeting is thus a mosaic of movements and words constituting affirmative thoughts and sentiments. In human society it is an approach mechanism, brimming with social, emotional and spiritual significance. In fact it is said that in Namaste the hands are put together like a knife so that people may cut through all differences that may exist, and immediately get to the shared ground that is common to all peoples of all cultures. In this context, a comparison with the widely prevalent 'handshake' is inevitable.

Though shaking hands is an extremely intimate gesture, Namaste scores over it in some ways. Primarily is the one that Namaste is a great equalizer. You do Namaste with God (and not shake hands!). A king or president cannot shake hands with the large multitude they are addressing. But Namaste serves the purpose. It is the same gesture one would have exchanged with a king when with him alone. So no incongruity arises. In the absence of Namaste, those facing a large audience will have to make do with a wave of the hands, a much less congenial greeting, and indeed which does not state the essential equality of all people, but highlights the difference even more. But on a parallel level it has been conjectured that both the Namaste and the handshake developed out of a desire on the part of both the parties to show themselves to be unarmed and devoid of malicious intention. The outstretched hand, and the palms joined together, both establish the proponents as disarmed and show that they come in peace.

As much as yoga is an exercise to bring all levels of our existence, including the physical and intellectual, in complete harmony with the rhythms of nature, the gesture of Namaste is a yoga in itself. It isn't surprising that any yogic activity begins with the performance of this deeply spiritual gesture.

The Buddhists went further and gave it the status of a mudra, that is, a gesture displayed by deities, where it was known as the Anjali mudra. The word Anjali itself is derived from the root Anj, meaning "to adorn, honor, celebrate or anoint." According to Indologist Renov "Meditation depends upon the relationship between the hands (mudras), the mouth (mantras) and the mind (yoga)".

The performance of Namaste is comprised of all these three activities. Thus Namaste is in essence equivalent to meditation, which is the language of our spirit in conversation with god, and the perfect vehicle for bathing us in the rivers of divine pleasure.

Extract from an article by Nitin Kumar, Editor of www.exoticindia.com

Natural forces within us are the healers of disease. ~ Hippocrates

6

New Possibilities with Reiki 2

"Be yourself; everyone else is already taken." — Oscar Wilde

The second degree brings new possibilities. After the initiation ceremony the second degree practitioner is taught how to use the sacred Reiki symbols.

These symbols are the keys that give the practitioner access to the full potential of the universal life force. There are three major new skills gained through the study of second degree Reiki.

They are as follows:

The Reiki practitioner can increase and focus the universal life force. This can be used for self healing or to heal others.

The Reiki practitioner can complete a full Reiki treatment in about 15 minutes compared to the 90 minutes normally required by a first degree practitioner. The Reiki practitioner can now help more people in less time.

The Reiki practitioner can send distant healing across time and space. Through the symbols the second degree practitioner can connect to another person or being anywhere in the universe — either in the past, present or in the future.

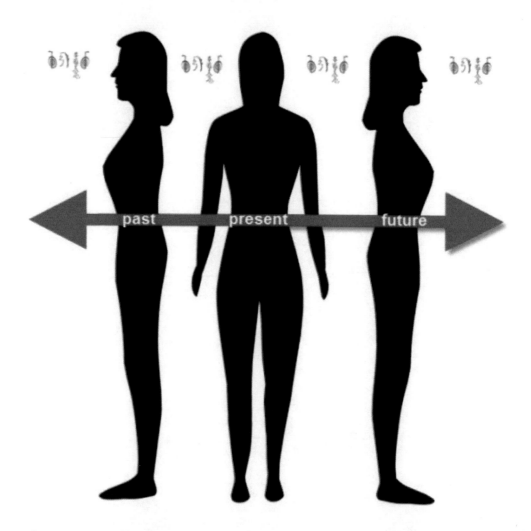

As you incorporate the Reiki symbols into your life you will find unlimited uses for them. The greater your understanding and imagination, the more varied applications you will discover and develop.

After the initiation ceremony the student will find that their personal vibratory level has heightened by as much as four times that of the first degree attunement. Their psychic abilities also increase by between 80-100%. As with all attunements the student will go through a 21 day detoxification process as their mind body and spirit finds equilibrium.

The more I learn, the more I live. – Anon

7

The Sacred Reiki Symbols

"There are only two ways to live your life. One is as though nothing is a miracle. The other is as though everything is a miracle." — Albert Einstein

The symbols are a very special, unique and important part of Reiki that help the Reiki Practitioner connect more effectively to the Universal Life Force. They are the keys that unlock the flow of Reiki and enhance and amplify the universal life force.

You can of course access the Reiki energy without the symbols, as taught in the first degree. However the Sacred Reiki Symbols are very important and can be harnessed by the Practitioner to strengthen and focus the reiki energy during a treatment session.

Dr Usui's four sacred symbols are known as the traditional Reiki symbols. The first three symbols are taught to students during the second degree, while the fourth and master symbol is taught to third degree reiki students. Students are initiated/attuned to the symbols during the Attunement ceremony. Once a student has been attuned to the Reiki symbols; like being attuned to reiki the student will be linked at a conscious and subconscious level to those symbols for life. Reiki will continue to flow even if you do not consciously used the symbols during a reiki session. As your understanding and appreciation of the Reiki develops through daily practice, you will be able to choose for yourself to what extent you use the symbols in your Practice.

It is important to remember that just like the Reiki Energy; the Reiki Symbols cannot do any harm. They can only be used for good.

During the attunement ceremony, the reiki master uses the symbols to transfer and link the sacred symbols with the reiki energy and the student; so the student from that point forward can either consciously or unconsciously draw upon this new amplified reiki energy quickly and easily to treat themselves and/or others in the future.

Once the second degree Usui Reiki student has studied and assimilated the first three reiki symbols, their healing abilities are immediately heightened. Without the second degree attunement however, the symbols will not work and are worthless.

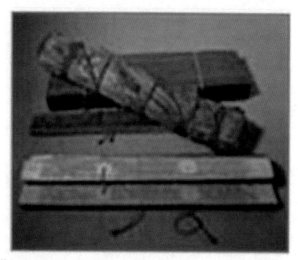

Mikao Usui originally taught Reiki without the use of symbols. However, he introduced them after a while to help his students better understand and more easily connect to the Reiki energy. Dr. Hayashi and Madam Takata both use symbols when they taught reiki to others. The Reiki symbols are now an integral part of studying reiki and are a very important part of the attunement ceremony.

The four symbols were found in the Sanskrit sutras by Dr Usui. He realised during his time of fasting and meditation on Mount Kurayama that these esoteric symbols would enable him and others to be finely tuned into Reiki, just like tuning a television or radio signal.

The symbols were the tools he needed to focus the Reiki energy, enabling him and others to bridge the gap between the healer and the recipient, across which the universal life force could be drawn and sent as necessary. These sacred symbols are also for self healing. They dissolve old destructive patterns, and increase the intuitive abilities of the student, while raising their conscious awareness and peace of mind to a new high.

Transcendental by nature, the Reiki symbols connect the practitioner and the recipient directly to the higher self or higher consciousness-the Rei. The symbols are similar to energy transformers they boost and expand the energy field. When a symbol is drawn or visualised in the outer realm it becomes a mirror image of another symbol on an inner realm. Simultaneously a connection occurs which has ramifications on all levels — inner and outer.

It is vitally important that at the moment of drawing the symbols the intention of the Reiki practitioner is absolutely clear and positive. Visualise or imagine the symbol as a live energy. Many see that energy as a white light. The symbols can be drawn mentally and transferred from the Reiki practitioner's third eye on to the various chakra and hand positions on the recipients' body.

Some Reiki practitioners draw the symbols on the roof of their mouth with their tongue before transferring the symbols to a recipient. While other Reiki practitioners; simply draw the symbols on their hands or the bodies of the recipient. *If you are going to draw them, ensure no-one sees them.*

"You may say I'm a dreamer, but I'm not the only one. I hope someday you'll join us. And the world will live as one." — *John Lennon*

8

The First Sacred Symbol
Cho Ku Rei

"What lies behind us and what lies before us are tiny matters compared to what lies within us." — Ralph Waldo Emerson

The first symbol is the Cho-Ku-Rei pronounced cho-koo-ray. It is the power symbol and the activator; often called "the light switch" as it turns on and activates all the other symbols.

CHO – To cut. Remove illusions in order to see the whole.

KU – Penetrating. Imagine a sword slicing through.

REI – Universal. Omnipresent, present everywhere.

The Cho-Ku-Rei cuts through and removes resistance. In Japanese Cho-Ku means imperial command — immediate. The esoteric meaning of the symbol is dis-creation, illness and disease are creations being constantly recreated.

How to draw the Cho-Ku-Rei

Cho Ku Rei

Stroke 1 – Draw a horizontal line from left to right.

Stroke 2 – Draw a vertical line from top to bottom.

Stroke 3 – Draw three and a half decreasing circles finishing on the vertical line as shown.

The Cho-Ku-Rei symbol dis-creates. This is the symbol that 'turns on' the second degree energy. Without this symbol the practitioner is still channelling only first degree energy. It can be used alone or as an activator for all the other symbols. Reiki's infinite wisdom will bring about whatever is needed.

How to Use the Cho-Ku-Rei Symbol

There are six main ways of transferring the Cho-Ku-Rei symbol from yourself onto your client. They are as follows:

Visualise or imagine a brilliant white Cho-Ku-Rei Symbol projected from your third eye chakra onto the back of your hands as you rest them on the different hand positions of your client.

Visualise or imagine a brilliant white Cho-Ku-Rei symbol on the palms of your hands before you place your hands onto your client.

Draw the Cho-Ku-Rei symbol on the roof of your mouth with your tongue. Then project the symbol onto the back of your hands as they rest on your client.

Draw the Cho-Ku-Rei symbol on the roof of your mouth with your tongue. Then project the symbol onto the palms of your hands before you place your hands onto your client.

Draw the Cho-Ku-Rei symbol onto the palms of your hands using your index fingers. Then place your hands onto your client.

Draw the Cho-Ku-Rei symbol in the air with your index finger in the direction you wish the Reiki to go.

Important Note - Never allow anyone to observe you drawing the symbols unless they are a second degree practitioner or a Reiki master.

To activate the symbols you have just drawn you must always silently intone the words Cho-Ku-Rei three times. The symbol will not work without the words silently intoned. If the situation calls for it write the problem down on a piece of paper and draw the Cho-Ku-Rei symbol over the top of the writing. Remember to silently intone the words Cho-Ku-Rei three times. Then place the paper in the palm of your hands for a few minutes.

Examples of Uses for the Cho-Ku-Rei (CKR) Symbol:

The CKR turns on the second degree Reiki energy.

The CKR activates all the other symbols.

The CKR protects you on all levels.

The CKR will bring about whatever is needed in a situation.

The CKR cleanses energies in your home, office, crystals, car etc.

The CKR brings balance into your life.

The CKR can be sewn into your children's clothes.

The CKR can be sent under a stamp on a letter.

The CKR can be placed under a sticker on a gift.

The CKR can be used on your food, drink, plants, animals etc.

The CKR can be used to help your career. Draw in on your desk, under the cash register, documents, letters, the telephone, your diary, computer, contract pads, tax or VAT forms.

The CKR can be used on airlines, trains, pilots, drivers etc.

The CKR can be drawn invisibly under your doormat, under wallpaper, in cupboards, behind pictures, on your front door.

You are only limited by your imagination. As you incorporate the symbols into your life you will use Reiki on everything.

The last place we tend to look for healing is within ourselves. ~ Wayne Muller

9

The Second Sacred Symbol
Sei Heiki

Happiness is not something ready made.
It comes from your own actions." — Dalai Lama XIV

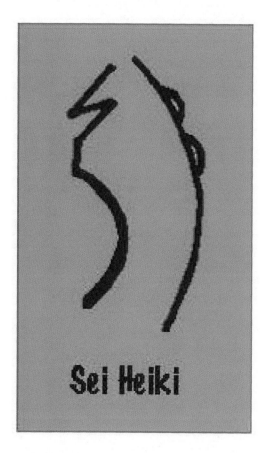

The second symbol is the Sei-Heiki pronounced say-high-key. This is the emotional and mental symbol used primarily for emotional and mental healing. Sei-Heiki balances the right and left brain.

SEI – means birth, coming into being.

HEIKI – means balance. Equilibrium.

How to draw the Sei-Heiki

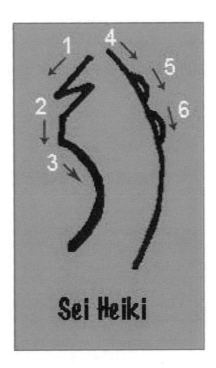

Stroke 1 – Draw a three part zigzag line as shown.

Stroke 2 -Draw a vertical line from top to bottom.

Stroke 3 – Draw a curved line from top to bottom.

Stroke 4 – Draw a curved line from top to bottom.

Stroke 5 & 6 – Draw two curved lines as shown from top to bottom.

How to Use the Sei-Heiki Symbol

There are six main ways of transferring the Sei-Heiki symbol from yourself onto your client. They are as follows:

Visualise or imagine a brilliant white Sei-Heiki Symbol projected from your third eye chakra onto the back of your hands as you rest them on the different hand positions of your client.

Visualise or imagine a brilliant white Sei-Heiki symbol on the palms of your hands before you place your hands onto your client.

Draw the Sei-Heiki symbol on the roof of your mouth with your tongue. Then project the symbol onto the back of your hands as they rest on your client.

Draw the Sei-Heiki symbol on the roof of your mouth with your tongue. Then project the symbol onto the palms of your hands before you place your hands onto your client.

Draw the Sei-Heiki symbol onto the palms of your hands using your index fingers. Then place your hands onto your client.

Draw the Sei-Heiki symbol in the air with your index finger in the direction you wish the Reiki to go.

Important Note - Never allow anyone to observe you drawing the symbols unless they are a second degree practitioner or a Reiki master.

To activate the Sei-Heiki symbol you must first draw the Cho-Ku-Rei intoning the words Cho-Ku-Rei three times. You then draw the Sei-Heiki on top of the Cho-Ku-Rei and intone the Words Sei-Heiki three times. Finally you draw the Cho-Ku-Rei on top of the Sei-Heiki remembering to intone the words Cho-Ku-Rei three more times. (See illustration below – the Reiki sandwich).

The Reiki Sandwich

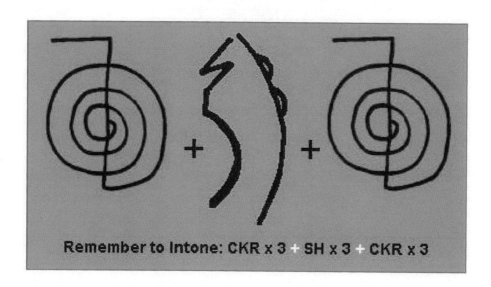

Remember to Intone: CKR x 3 + SH x 3 + CKR x 3

In a situation where you feel your client is suffering from some sort of emotional or mental block the Reiki sandwich shown above can be used to release any blockages and allow the healing process to begin.

Visualise or imagine the Reiki sandwich coming out of your third eye chakra and entering the third eye chakra of your client. As you intone the words add the rider if it be for the highest good. Alternatively, draw the symbols on your hands and then place them over the clients' third eye chakra.

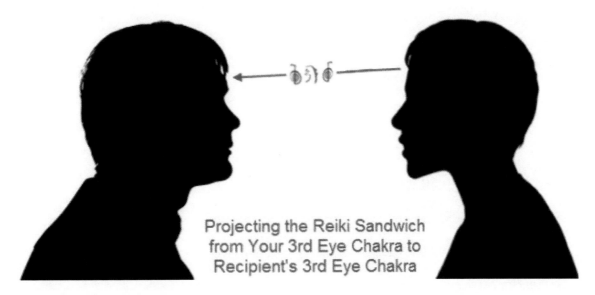

Projecting the Reiki Sandwich
from Your 3rd Eye Chakra to
Recipient's 3rd Eye Chakra

This is often needed when you are treating a person for addictions, weight loss or unwanted habits. Keep a box of tissues handy as this can often cause the client to become weepy and emotional.

The Reiki sandwich can be used on all the normal hand positions. However, the third eye chakra position must be treated with the utmost care and responsibility. The Reiki sandwich will take the practitioner deep into the clients mind. It is vitally important to guard your thoughts as they can be picked up by the client. Ask the higher self of your client for consent before working on their third eye chakra. Your own intuition will give you the answer.

If you are treating a person who is suffering from a disease such as cancer, leukaemia or Aids visualise thousands of Sei-Heiki symbols penetrating every cell in your clients' body.

When you find something you do not understand or you have a question that needs answering. Write it down on a piece of paper and draw the Reiki sandwich shown on the previous page over the top of it. Your answer will come to you intuitively.

Examples of Uses for the Sei-Heiki (SH) Symbol:

The SH works on blockages and resistance in the body.

The SH works on long-standing problems.

The SH works on drink, drugs and smoking addictions.

The SH works on anorexia nervosa and bulimia.

The SH works on relationship problems.

The SH works on nervousness, fear, phobias.

The SH works on anger, sadness and other emotions.

The SH works on grief from bereavement.

The SH works on improving memory.

The SH works on enhancing affirmations.

The SH works on improving intuition and inspiration.

The SH works on calming negative atmospheres.

The SH balances energies in your home, work, crystals.

The SH works on calming arguments.

The SH works on improving poor communications.

The SH protects you on every level.

The SH Protects you from the losing personal belongings.

The SH protects you while travelling.

The SH helps you find lost articles.

The SH improves creativity.

The SH helps with coma patients, head injuries.

The SH works on others as well as yourself.

Never use Reiki to manipulate others. Misuse is one way of losing your gift.

When we need these healing times, there is nothing better than a good long walk. It is amazing how the rhythmic movements of the feet and legs are so intimately attached to cobweb cleaners in the brain. ~ Anne Wilson Schaef

10

The Third Sacred Symbol
Hon Sha Ze Sho Nen

"God doesn't require us to succeed; he only requires that you try." — Mother Teresa

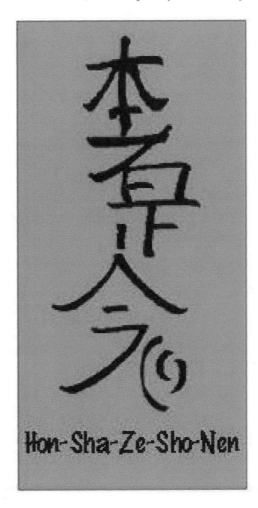

The third Usui symbol is the Hon-Sha-Ze-Sho-Nen. This symbol is known as the distant or absent healing symbol, and is used to transcend time and space – past present and future. Like all the other Symbols the Cho-Ku-Rei symbol is used first to activate the Hon-Sha-Ze-Sho-Nen.

The HSZSN gives the Reiki practitioner the ability to channel Reiki across space, distance becomes no object. Reiki can be sent to a person across the room in a therapy situation or channelled to a person in another part of the world.

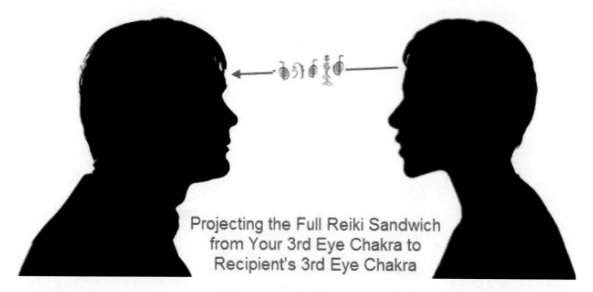

Projecting the Full Reiki Sandwich
from Your 3rd Eye Chakra to
Recipient's 3rd Eye Chakra

The HSZSN also allows the practitioner to bridge time from the present to the past or future. Reiki can be sent back to heal a childhood problem or even further still to a past life.

Future situations such as operations, interviews or business meetings can be greatly improved by sending Reiki in advance. Time has no relevance when the HSZSN symbol is used.

How to Draw the Hon-Sha-Ze-Sho-Nen Symbol

When the Hon-Sha-Ze-Sho-Nen symbol is drawn all strokes are drawn from left to right and from top to bottom.

1 The first horizontal stroke means number one; the beginning. Eternity begins in the moment.

2 The second vertical stroke which crosses over the first one; means number ten. The End. Completion. The Japanese only count up to ten.

3/4 The third and fourth strokes combined with strokes one and two symbolise a tree in Japanese.

Esoterically it means the tree of life; also the tree of death and transformation, of knowledge, evil, desire and resistance. It also represents the tree of timelessness- it cannot die because it was never born.

5 The fifth horizontal stroke means the root – the root of the tree. The cause; the essence, the origin.

Strokes one to five combined form the first kanji – HON. (Kanji means Japanese writing using Chinese characters. Kan – Chinese, Ji – character).

Sha

6 The sixth horizontal stroke symbolises the land – the earth.

7 Stroke seven a downward curving line means becomes – existence.

8 Stroke eight is a vertical line drawn downwards from the curved line.

9 Stroke nine is drawn from the left and curves sharply downwards as shown.(Strokes eight and nine combined look similar to a lowercase letter 'n').

10 Stroke ten is a horizontal line drawn from the centre of stroke eight. The strokes eight, nine and ten form another Kanji which translated means the sun.

Here we have the sun under the earth. Light coming into existence – the sun about to rise. Strokes six through to ten forms the Kanji – SHA which means a person that creates -i.e. a potter. A potter produces a vase from a lump of clay. He reveals the vase that was hidden in the clay. This symbol means what was hidden is brought into being. Bringing light onto the earth. The miracle of Reiki – when you place your hands on someone, you are revealing little by little what is already there.

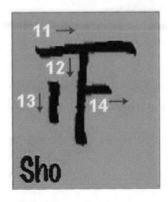

Sho

11 Stroke number eleven is a horizontal line drawn from left to right and seals the SHA kanji.

12 Stroke number twelve is a vertical line drawn from the centre of stroke eleven downwards.

13 Stroke number thirteen is a vertical line drawn as shown.

14 Stroke number fourteen is a horizontal line drawn as shown.

Strokes eleven to fourteen form the next kanji – SHO which means right, correct, justice.

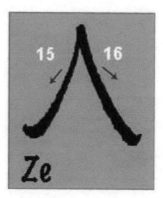

15 Stroke number fifteen curves downwards to the left as shown.

16 Stroke number sixteen curves downwards to the right as shown.

Stroke fifteen and sixteen combined form the kanji – ZE; which means harmony. Acting appropriately; in the correct manner. Remember energy with intelligence, it always goes where it is needed.

Although the kanji ZE is drawn after the SHO it is spoken before it.

17 Stroke number seventeen is a horizontal line drawn from left to right as shown.

18 Stroke number eighteen is drawn horizontally from left to right parallel to stroke number seventeen. It then curves downwards and to the left as shown.

19 Stroke nineteen curves downwards similar to the letter 'C' as shown.

20 Stroke twenty also curves downwards similar to the letter 'C' as shown.

21 Finally, stroke number twenty-one also curves downwards as shown.

Strokes seventeen to twenty-one form the final kanji – NEN which means the heart, thought, also now – in the present moment in time.

How to Use the Hon-Sha-Ze-Sho-Nen Symbol

There are six main ways of transferring the Hon-Sha-Ze-Sho-Nen symbol from yourself onto your client. They are as follows:

Visualise or imagine a brilliant white Hon-Sha-Ze-Sho-Nen Symbol projected from your third eye chakra onto the back of your hands as you rest them on the different hand positions of your client.

Visualise or imagine a brilliant white Hon-Sha-Ze-Sho-Nen symbol on the palms of your hands before you place your hands onto your client.

Draw the Hon-Sha-Ze-Sho-Nen symbol on the roof of your mouth with your tongue. Then project the symbol onto the back of your hands as they rest on your client.

Draw the Hon-Sha-Ze-Sho-Nen symbol on the roof of your mouth with your tongue. Then project the symbol onto the palms of your hands before you place your hands onto your client.

Draw the Hon-Sha-Ze-Sho-Nen symbol onto the palms of your hands using your index fingers. Then place your hands onto your client.

Draw the Hon-Sha-Ze-Sho-Nen symbol in the air with your index finger in the direction you wish the Reiki to go.

Important Note - Never allow anyone to observe you drawing the symbols unless they are a second degree practitioner or a Reiki Master.

To activate the Hon-Sha-Ze-Sho-Nen symbol you must first draw the Cho-Ku-Rei intoning the words Cho-Ku-Rei three times. You then draw the Hon-Sha-Ze-Sho-Nen on top of the Cho-Ku-Rei and intone the Words Hon-Sha-Ze-Sho-Nen three times. Finally you draw the Cho-Ku-Rei on top of the Hon-Sha-Ze-Sho-Nen remembering to intone the words Cho-Ku-Rei three more times. (See illustration below – the Reiki sandwich).

The Full Reiki Sandwich

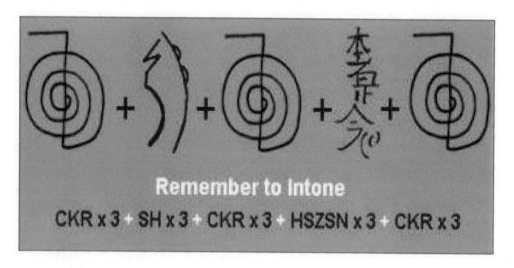

Remember to Intone
CKR x 3 + SH x 3 + CKR x 3 + HSZSN x 3 + CKR x 3

Examples of Uses for the HSZSN Symbol:

The HSZSN works on deep seated diseases.

The HSZSN works on long standing problems.

The HSZSN channels Reiki to a person in another country.

The HSZSN channels Reiki to someone in hospital.

The HSZSN works on groups or large organisations.

The HSZSN works on towns, cities and countries.

The HSZSN channels Reiki to disaster or crisis situations.

The HSZSN channels Reiki to world leaders.

The HSZSN works on driving tests and examinations.

The HSZSN works on interviews and meetings.

The HSZSN works on karmic past life issues.

The HSZSN works on children while they sleep or rest.

The HSZSN helps treat patients with burns who cannot be touched or where there is a risk of infection through touch.

The HSZSN heals the inner child.

The HSZSN heals the past present and future.

The HSZSN works on world peace.

You are only limited by your imagination. Believe and succeed.

There is nothing quite so satisfying, and so healing, as a good cry. ~ Leo Buscaglia

11

Distant or Absent Reiki Healing

"It's not what you look at that matters, it's what you see." — Henry David Thoreau

The three Usui Reiki symbols are the keys that unlock the doors to absent and distance healing. It is important to study and master these symbols.

Practice drawing them until you can draw and visualise all three of them without referring to these pages.

There are many ways to channel Reiki through the symbols. As you begin to practice and work with the symbols you will discover which method you prefer. It is not important to understand how it works. Belief and the right attitude make the real difference. Leave the logical sceptical part of your brain to one side and experience through practice how powerful and effective absent and distance healing can be.

A wonderful way to prove to your self that it works is to send distance healing to a friend's sick pet. Animals are not influenced by hype. When you discover how you were able to treat an animal by sending Reiki through the symbols you will remove any doubts about its validity and concentrate on perfecting this profound form of healing.

Preparing to Send Distant Reiki Healing

With practice you'll be able to send Reiki Healing Energy at will, whenever it's required. You will be able to perform a distant healing session no matter what the environment or location you find yourself in or no matter what distractions may be around you at that time. You will have the ability through practice to simple filter out everything else and focus in on the job at hand – sending reiki to a person, place or event etc. This ability can be extremely useful especially if you need to send reiki in the event of an emergency and you find yourself out shopping, or at work or at a sporting event etc. for example.

Initially when you first practice distant healing try to follow these guidelines below to help you connect and perform the healing session correctly. Find a quiet place and ensure you have enough time so you won't be interrupted. You need to focus on the following:

Decide on the Distant Healing method you are going to use to send reiki before you begin the session so you can when ready smoothly perform the distant healing for the recipient.

Begin by grounding yourself and connecting with the Reiki – The Universal Life Force: Just like an in-person Reiki session, you need to connect with Reiki so that you are in the best position mentally and spiritually to channel Reiki. If you need to please review the Essence of Reiki 1 Lesson 9 – Preparing to Treat Others with reiki.

Remember to remove the Ego – You are Just the Channel for Reiki; which will be doing the work and will be travelling across time and space to connect with the recipient of the distant healing. Ensure you feel the flow of Reiki before you connect with the recipient and start sending reiki to them.

Once you feel the connection with the Universal Life Force, start transmitting the healing Reiki energy using the method you had earlier decided upon. Remember all methods will work, so try them all so you can decide on your favourite method/s to use in the future.

Keep the distant healing session going for as long as you intuitively feel it should continue. It makes no difference whether it lasts 5 minutes or an hour; reiki will go where it is needed and continue to work even after you have closed the session down. An average distant healing session lasts about 15 minutes. There is no right or wrong in distant reiki, the KEY as always is in the INTENTION.

Always end the Reiki distant healing session with a positive envisioning of the person, place, event or situation you focus on. Go ahead and imagine a different scenario for your past. After all, your past influences your thoughts and emotions; allow Reiki to influence your thoughts and emotions in a new, inspired way.

After your distant healing session, release the outcome to the Infinite Wisdom and Infinite Love, or Spirit of Reiki. Your intellect may know or not know what the best possible outcome is; but Reiki always knows!

Make sure you remember to disconnect from the recipient once the session is completed and wash your hands in cold running water if possible depending on your location. Also drink a glass of cold water to help ground yourself.

Popular Methods Used to Send Distant Reiki Healing

When you first practice Distant Healing it is always best to follow a pre-arranged format that you feel comfortable with so you can remain relaxed and focussed on the healing session rather than the mechanics of what you are doing.

Practice makes permanent. Like learning to drive a car, in the beginning it can seem overwhelming to think about all the things you need to do and remember to keep the car on the road safely. Within a short space of time you through repetition and practice you permanently encode the mechanics of driving in to your subconscious and you can then enjoy the experience of driving. Likewise, once you have mastered the mechanics of performing a distant healing session you will be able to just relax and focus of the healing session and not on what you need to do next – it will all become automatic. As you grow in confidence, you can begin to rely more on your intuition to guide you during your future distant reiki healing sessions.

Because you don't have the recipient in front of you when you are performing the Distant Healing, you need to find a way to "see" what is going on during the session. Listed below are a number of substitute methods you can use to help you visualize or represent the distant Reiki recipient in your mind.

The Surrogate Method

You can literally use anything as a surrogate to channel Reiki. The most important thing you must do is clearly specify that the surrogate is taking the place of whoever or whatever you are sending Reiki to during your invocation. A photograph, cushions, dolls, teddy bears, pens, crystals or the details of the person or thing written on a piece of paper are all good examples of a surrogate.

Many Reiki practitioners have their favourite surrogate and use it for all their distance and absent healing. If you have a soft toy that you cherish try using that. A ball or small globe can be used as a surrogate to channel Reiki to mother earth. We always Reiki our car before each journey; by using the cars steering wheel as a surrogate for the car. When we treat people using a surrogate we prefer to use a teddy bear as we are able to work more precisely on the various hand positions and chakra's. For example if a person has a sore or injure left leg we spend more time treating the surrogate teddy bears left leg.

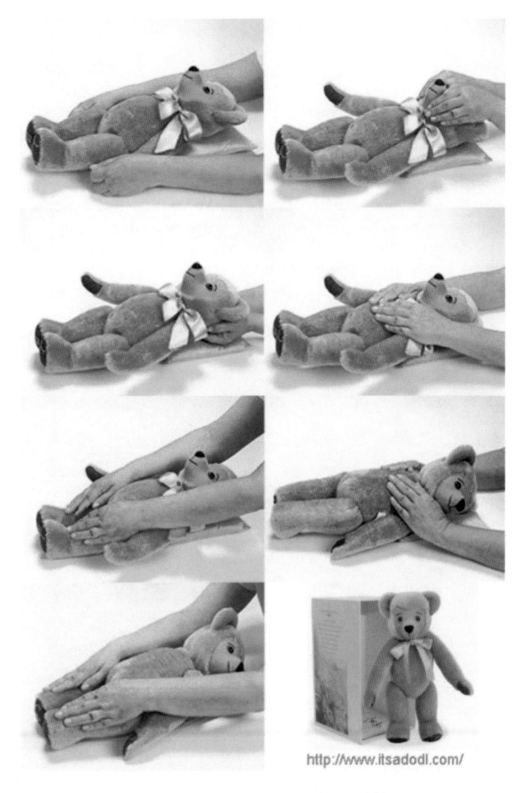

Let us assume for example you want to channel Reiki to your mother who is in hospital in another part of the country or world. Find a photograph of your mother. Write down her name, the hospital she has been admitted to and the hospital ward or room number on a piece of paper. Telephone your mother and ask for her permission to send healing to her. Choose a time between yourselves when you both will be able to relax and won't be disturbed. Place the photo and the piece of paper in your hands. If no-one is able to see or hear you make your normal invocation aloud adding also that the photo and piece of paper are to be used as a surrogate for your mother.

A rider is similar to a caveat. When we are calling upon reiki the universal life force to help heal our friend/client etc we must remember that we do not control or have any say on what is in the best interest for that client/friend etc – we remove our ego and let reiki and its infinite wisdom do what is needed based on the clients best interest – not our perceptions of what is best for them.

So the rider hands responsibility back to reiki to do what is needed and go where it is needed. Sometimes you will discover in your future reiki practice that it is not the right time for whatever higher reason for that person to receive healing. This can be frustrating especially if the person you want to send healing to is a close family member or friend, but you must respect their higher self's reasons for not accepting or wanting healing; so you MUST always try to ask permission first before you send anyone healing or at least add the Rider – Should it be for their higher good.

Focus your attention on your mother and visualise or imagine her lying in her hospital bed or sitting in a chair depending on what you have arranged with her. Holding the photo and piece of paper in your non dominant hand; draw the Full Reiki Sandwich over the top with your dominant hand. Remember to intone the symbols and add the rider if it be for the highest good. Close your hands together and imagine sending healing light to your mother. Keep your hands closed for at least five minutes. As you become more experienced you will be able to intuitively work with the differing energy levels.

Once you have sent the Reiki take a moment to visualise or imagine your mother getting better. See her leave the hospital and making a full recovery. Trust in the power and wisdom of Reiki to make your vision into a reality. Complete the treatment by thanking the universal life force and any guides or helpers who assisted you in the treatment.

Remember the recipient is drawing the Reiki and doing the healing, you are just a channel. They need to be aware and ready to work with you in the healing process. Make sure they take the time each day to relax and are open to receiving Reiki.

If the recipient is not able to spend too much time relaxing each day you can specify an agreed time for the Reiki treatment to last. All you need to do is write down the agreed length of time for the treatment on the piece of paper. This process like the normal full hands on treatment should be repeated at least four times over four consecutive days. To save yourself time you can set up the four healing sessions in one go. Simply write on a piece of paper in addition to the recipients name and address the time and dates you wish the Reiki to be channelled to them You will only need to spend one five or ten minutes session channelling Reiki to your client so they receive it over four different days.

Remember the symbols transcend time and space. As long as the recipient takes the time each day to tune into your Reiki signal they will receive and benefit from the universal life force.

Obviously the stronger your intent and the more time you spend sending Reiki the stronger and more profound it will be. Like all of the treatments the more practice and experience you gain the easier and stronger it will get.

The Thigh and Knee Method

Another method often used for absent or distance healing is the thigh and knee method. You will need to be seated to perform this treatment. Make your right knee and thigh the surrogate for the head and front of your client. Your right knee is your client head, your right mid thigh is your clients' body and the rest of your right thigh is your clients legs and feet. The left knee and thigh represents the back of your clients head and body. Your left knee is the back of your clients head, your left mid thigh is your clients back and the rest of your left thigh represents the back of your clients' legs and feet.

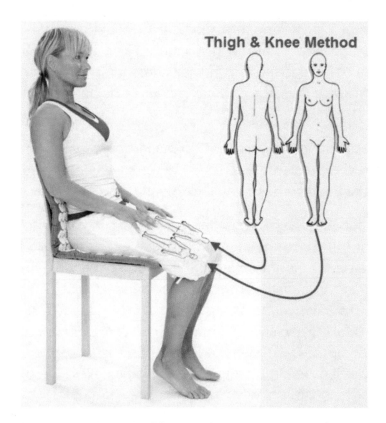

This treatment takes approximately fifteen minutes to complete. Using your left hand for the left knee and thigh and your right hand for the right knee and thigh; work on the three positions for about five minutes each. Draw, visualise or imagine the three Usui symbols (The Full Reiki Sandwich) on each hand position. Remember to intone the words of each symbol three times. Complete the treatment as normal by thanking the universal life force and finally sweep your clients aura by rubbing your knees and thighs.

Thigh and Knee Method

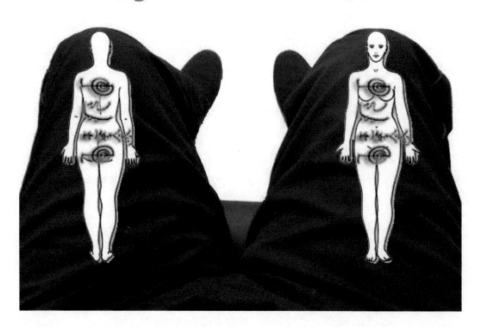

Visualisation Techniques

There are two basic ways of using visualisation to perform absent or distance healing. The first involves visualising or imagining the person you wish to treat with Reiki. For example, let's assume you want to treat a close friend who is in hospital.

Close your eyes and make your invocation. Repeat your friends name three times to focus your mind and establish a connection between yourself and your friend in hospital. Transport your friend from the hospital and visualise or imagine them in a miniature form resting in the palms of your hands. Open your eyes and project the symbols from your third eye onto your friend resting in the palms of your hands. Alternatively, you can place your friend in one hand and draw the symbols over your friend with the other hand. Remember to intone the words three times and add the rider should it be for the highest good.

Gently cup your hands together. Keep your hands close for five to ten minutes or until you intuitively feel the treatment is complete. Open your hands and visualise or imagine your friend making a full recovery. Visualise or imagine a healing light enveloping your friend. Close your eyes and transport your friend back to the hospital. Say goodbye leaving the healing light with them to continue and complete the healing process. Complete the treatment by thanking the universal life force and make sure to wash your hands in cold running water.

Alternative Visualisation Technique

For this example let's assume you want to treat a friend's child who has chickenpox. If you also have children you probably don't want to risk infecting them by treating your friends' child in person. Close your eyes and visualise or imagine being in your friends home. Have the child lie down on a bed or couch. Make your invocation and then project the three Usui symbols onto the child. Conduct a full reiki hands on treatment.

Visualise or imagine a healing light enveloping the child. Say goodbye leaving the healing light with them to continue and complete the healing process. Complete the treatment by thanking the universal life force. Return to your home or office. Open your eyes. Remember to wash your hands under cold running water.

Before healing others, heal yourself ~ Anon

12

A Traditional Distant Reiki Healing Technique

"The biggest adventure you can ever take is to live the life of your dreams." — Oprah Winfrey

Important Note: Whenever you perform distant Reiki healing, your intuition or imagination is particularly useful because you won't receive instant feedback directly from the recipient during the session. Unlike an in person treatment you can't observe or experience exactly what the distant recipient is going through; so you will not be able to see (intuitively imagine) if that person is sighing, crying, smiling, coughing or pick up on any of the more subtle non-verbal communications/responses like involuntary movements or a change in skin tone for example.

The Structure of a Traditional

Reiki Distant Healing Session

Step 1: Ask For Permission To Send The Distant Healing to the Recipient.

When you are treating someone in person with Reiki, it is safe to assume that you have their permission to treat them with Reiki otherwise why would they be there! However, when we perform a Distant Reiki Treatment we need to ensure that wherever possible (they may be seriously ill and unable to talk to you) we have the recipient's or a close family member of the recipient, permission to channel reiki to them so we can maintain good ethical practice and integrity.

The decision of whether to send reiki healing to someone no matter how in need you may think they are must remain wherever possible with the individual. Don't force your good intentions to channel healing on someone else against their will. If your offer of Reiki is refused by one person, you can always find someone who does want to receive the Reiki healing energy.

Normally, you will find that a person in need of healing will contact you with their request for reiki healing. The request may come in an email, a note, a text, via your website, or verbally during a meeting or phone conversation. Their approach requesting distant healing is your green light, giving you permission to send Reiki.

Sometimes you'll receive a request for distant Reiki healing on another's behalf. If you aren't sure of the person's consent, you can choose to take one of the following courses of action:

If you have decided never to send Reiki to anyone unless they request it personally you could simply refuse to send Reiki. (We wouldn't personally recommend this option). Using Reiki Connect with the person and get their consent intuitively. You can do this by Meditating, and creating a picture in your mind of the person whom you want to connect with. Be in the room with them and ask them the question in your mind: "Do you want to receive long-distance Reiki from me?" If you get a clear yes or no, then proceed accordingly.

If you get an urgent or desperate request on another person's behalf ("please help my father, son, or Sister who is suffering from X disease"), you can use the intuitive approach to see if you can proceed or if you need to proceed immediately add the rider before you send the reiki to them – Should it be for their highest good.

You can also send Reiki with a specific intent so that it flows only where it is desired. In other words you can send Reiki without explicit approval, but first make clear in your mind that, if the person in question doesn't want Reiki, the energy will go to the earth or to some other person who wants it. You might say, "I am sending this energy to Mary, but if she doesn't want or need it, let it go to someone or some event/situation that does need it."

You may have strong feelings one way or another about getting permission to send Reiki. Follow what feels right for you – remember these are only guidelines. All over the world, people pray for one another without necessarily asking if the recipient wants that prayer. Some practitioners use this logic to send Reiki without getting permission. But most agree that the path of most integrity requires getting permission.

Step 2: The Traditional Distant Reiki Technique

Below is the basic reiki distant healing method we were taught using a photograph by our Reiki Master. Remember it is a guide; try lots of different methods until you find the one that you like the most or you intuitively feel gets the best results for you and your client.

Confirm you have the recipients' permission to send distant reiki healing

Holding the Photo of the recipient in your cupped hands (image pointing up towards your face) Visually draw on to that photo while intoning the names of the following symbols aloud three times each to create a virtual Reiki Sandwich:

Cho Ku Rei (Power symbol)

Sei Hei Ki (Emotional symbol)

Hon Sha Ze Sho Nen (Distance symbol)

Cho Ku Rei (Power symbol)

Say aloud the name of the receiving person three times as you close your hands gently together to cover the photo.

Now imagine being in the room with that person so you can see/imagine the recipient in your mind sitting or lying down ready to receive the treatment.

Now visually draw the virtual reiki sandwich on to the body of the recipient, once again intoning the name of the symbols three times.

Conduct a full Reiki session in your mind exactly as you would in person. You can speed up the process so it only takes a few minutes to complete the treatment in your mind. Remember to pay special attention to any known disease hot spots or places you are intuitively drawn to on the recipients' body.

Once the full treatment is completed; end the session by cleansing the recipients aura and ground them.

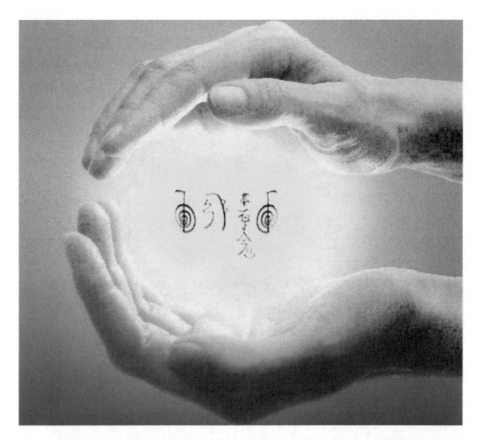

Once again this is only a guide. You will come across lots of different reiki practitioners and master/teachers that will offer different variations on every Reiki technique including Distant Healing.

As always Intention is the key to success, there is no right or wrong way!

Interestingly, Dr Mikao Usui's preferred distant healing method, which he called Enkaku Chiryo Ho. (Enkaku translates to "remote or sending," Chiryo to "treatment," and Ho to "method.") uses the visualizing technique of photographs, if available, to send Reiki to people at a distance, even if the distance is just another room in the same building.

Now wash your hands in cold running water and Ground yourself. Remember to thank reiki and your guides etc for participating in the distant healing session.

The most important medicine is tender love and care. – Mother Teresa

13

Examples of Sending Distant Reiki Healing

"Whether you live to be 50 or 100 makes no difference, if you made no difference in the world." — Jarod Kintz

As we know from our study of First Degree Reiki; When we think about using Reiki on ourselves or others we know Reiki will automatically start to flow through us as Reiki Practitioners. We can channel or Focus the reiki energy by either placing our hands on or above ourselves or someone else.

One of the most exciting things about becoming a Reiki 2 Practitioner is we now move in to a whole new realm of Reiki, where the restrictions of time, space and distance no longer exist. We have the power, tools and techniques as Advanced Practitioners to send reiki to A Person, Group and even a Whole Country or Continent even if we are located on the other side of the world. In fact we can now channel reiki to the Past, Present or a Future Event or Situation.

In this Lesson we are going to discuss some of the different situations where you may want or be required to send distant Reiki using the methods you learnt in the previous lesson. Just imagine how exciting, rewarding, cathartic and possibly even life changing it could be to be able to send Reiki to every corner of the planet, to your own or others past, present and future to heal people, events, places and things.

Send Reiki Distantly to People

The majority of distant Reiki healing sessions will involve you sending reiki to another person over either a short or long distance. The recipient may be at their home or in a hospital in another country suffering from an illness or they may be simply in need of a energy boost or some relief from a stressful situation. The distance doesn't matter; it could be a mile away or 12,000 miles away on the other side of the world because Reiki can transcend any distance.

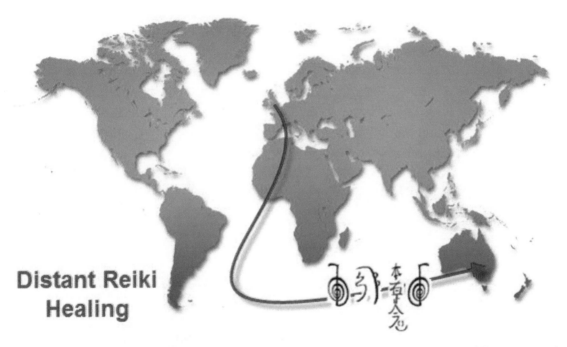

Distant Reiki Healing

When you send distant Reiki, you can also set the time it is received. For example, say you live in the UK and you wish to send reiki to a relative in Australia. It could be Monday morning in the UK (8 a.m. GMT) and you know your Relative is going into hospital for an operation the next day, Tuesday morning at 10 a.m. (Australian Local Time). With the time difference you will be in bed or too tired or concerned to send Reiki in the middle of the night. The solution is simple with Distant Reiki. You can sit down before the event (surgery) when you are relaxed and able to focus and simply ask the power and wisdom of reiki harnessing the power of the HSZSN symbol to deliver reiki to your relative at the time of the operation. In this way, you combine the features of crossing both time and space during the distant Reiki session.

Send Reiki to the Future

Reiki can be sent into the future ahead of time to important events such as a wedding, a driving test, exams, competitions, job interviews, doctor or dental appointments etc. Because you may not always be available at a particular time to send Reiki to someone or even yourself, this technique is a wonderful way to ensure that the power of Reiki is flowing at that special event to help you or the recipient should it be for your/their higher good.

When you send the Reiki, you can state the time and place and person who is to receive the Reiki and the situation if you know that information. For example, if you wanted to send Reiki to your teenage daughter who was about to sit a number of important exams over a period of 3 weeks so they could get the results they require for entrance into their chosen College/University; you could use their printed copy of their exam timetable and a photo of your daughter as the surrogate. Place the surrogate items in your hands, draw/visualise the reiki sandwich on the documents and state something like: "I ask that the power and wisdom of reiki is in and around my daughter (insert name) as she sits and takes the following examinations (insert dates and times of exams) at her (insert name of school) high school located at (insert address of school). I ask that the loving healing light of Reiki brings calm, clarity and focus to her so she can achieve her desired examination results and gain access to (insert name of college/university). I also ask that Reiki envelopes her with a bubble of healing white light protecting her from the negative energy of any fellow students in and around her in the examination room.

It is important to point out that in the example above, the daughter would have still needed to revise and prepare properly for the examinations. Reiki will of course bring calm and focus and the correct state of mind to the daughter, but it won't answer the questions for her.

Send Reiki to the Past

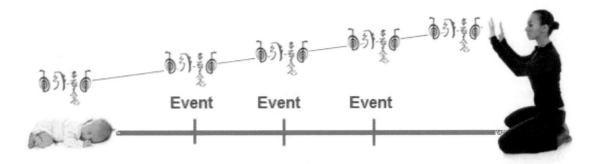

Event   Event   Event

The ability to send healing backward in time allows you to help heal previous events, experiences and situations. Of course sending reiki back along a person's timeline will not change history, but you can heal what results from it. People tend to hold onto past experiences, both good and bad, much of the healing done in the present time or now is actually healing the baggage carried forward from the past. For example, suppose that you have been suffering for years from a pain in your knee from a past sporting injury. You can return to the scene of the break/accident in your imagination and send Reiki to yourself. Doing so requires good use of imagination and visualization. Set your clear intention for the specific past experience or time period you want to focus on for the Reiki session. Remember you can send Reiki to a single moment in time (the moment you were born), or to a period of time (the two weeks your gran-mother was in the hospital).

Send Reiki to Yourself

You can use distant Reiki in your own life and on yourself in a number of ways including:

Your Past: Send Reiki back along your timeline (your past) to events or situations where you experienced pain or suffering or even a break up or loss. Sending healing reiki energy to those trying times in the past can bring relief and remove any blockages that maybe affecting you now in the present. Healing the past can be both cathartic and liberating and open up a whole new brighter future for you. In you are going to work on past events remember the box of tissues as you may stir up emotions and begin to cry as part of the process.

Your Present: You could be tired and run down and in need of a energy boost. Take a break, maybe even meditate for a few minutes and send reiki to yourself by imagining yourself in your mind's eye, see yourself sending reiki to yourself and then see and experience the beautiful healing white light of reiki energy envelope your whole body entering your crown chakra and bathing every muscle cell tissue and organ of your body with healing reiki energy.

Your Future: Send Reiki to your future self. Go one day, week, month or even years into your future. Think of a certain upcoming event in your future such as a vacation, retirement, and wedding or just send to the future with no event or time frame in mind asking reiki to guide you in your future reiki practice so you attract success and happiness to yourself.

Sometimes when you send Reiki to yourself in the past, present or future you will receive a message, an acknowledgement or validation. This may manifest in a positive sound or voice in your head, an image of a successful conclusion to the reason why you sent reiki to the event/situation or you may notice/sense a new feeling of calm or positivity. You can use any technique on yourself. In fact, it's best to put yourself first in order to learn and practice any technique but also so that you gain the benefits of Reiki healing.

Send Reiki to Places, Situations
and World Events or Disasters

Reiki can be sent to any place, situation, event or disaster area anywhere in the world. Reiki can be sent for example to:

You can send reiki distant energy to Mother Earth, which is itself receptive to healing. Hardly a week goes by without some form of disaster being beamed into our homes via 24 hour news channels with images of natural events that harm the earth including tropical storms, tsunamis, fires, volcanoes and earthquake's; and man-made disasters like forest fires, unnecessary pollution, destruction of rain forests and delicate eco-systems or the illegal poaching of endangered wildfire or whaling. Mother Earth provides us with every basic need we have for sustenance. It is only right that we treat this wonderful planet of ours with love and respect so when you can consider giving something back by sending reiki healing to the earth. You can send Reiki to the earth in a general way, and the energy can be taken where needed. Or you can send Reiki to specific places on earth, such as a continent, ocean, forest, or wherever you are drawn to send the energy.

You can also help to heal conflicts and major accidents or mindless attacks such as the following:

Road, Rail or Air Traffic accidents: Next time you hear of an accident or pass an accident on the road, you can send Reiki to all the people involved.

War Zones: Send Reiki to all the victims of War with an intention of bringing about a peaceful resolution and reconciliation.

Terrorist Attacks: Unfortunately we share the planet with some mindless groups and individuals with their own warped sense of reality. Send Reiki to all the victims and the relatives and friends of mindless terrorist attacks.

Political situations: During contentious elections or meetings of powerful groups that can have an impact of millions of people or even the world like the G8 or the UN, you can send Reiki so that the differences among political parties of different ideologies are healed and decisions are made that benefit the higher good of all humanity.

When you send Reiki to any of these situations listed above you will use the same techniques you use in any other distant Reiki session. It would be impossible to get permission from everyone involved in such an event or situation, so to preserve your integrity and ethical standpoint about only sending reiki if you are asked or have received permission to do so; you can intend that Reiki go to all who want it. You're not sending Reiki to any particular individual but making this healing energy available to those who need it most.

If you want to practice sending distant Reiki and don't know where to start, just open the newspaper or turn on a TV news programme. You will unfortunately be able to find lots of candidates to practice on.

Send Reiki to Multiple People/Events/Situations

As your Reiki Practice develops and you become busier; with more Reiki treatments. Workshops or requests for distant reiki you will need to find creative ways to juggle the workload. One of the ways you can save time while still providing great service to your clients is to send healing regularly to multiple People and/or Events and Situations. For example you may have several clients overseas who want you to send reiki to them every day for a month plus others asking you to send reiki to events in the future like weddings etc. Obviously it would be difficult and too time consuming to provide this service to everyone at separate times so you will need to combine several requests together and send reiki to them at the same time.

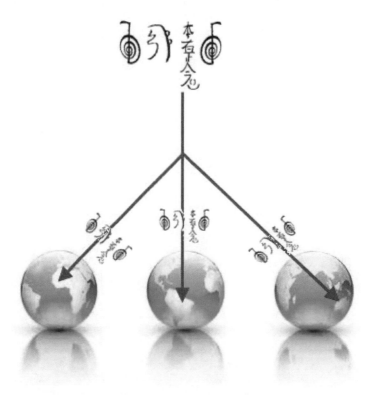

It's a bit like typing up and sending an email to one client and then retyping the same note and sending that to the second client and repeating the process for multiple clients – it could take you all day. As a time saver you can simply create a generic email, use mail merge software or the CC (carbon copy) function on your email client and in one go send multiple emails to clients all over the world at the same time saving you lots of effort and work while at the same time providing the information to all of your clients – a definite Win-Win. Sending Reiki to multiple clients is exactly the same thing, you get to help more people while at the same time being able to manage your time – A Win-Win.

You can send distant Reiki to lots of people/events etc in a number of creative ways including:

Reiki box: Write down the names of the people or situations you are sending healing to including any times and dates and put the card/paper with the names into a box along with any photographs if applicable. Reiki the box regularly and you send Reiki to all requests inside the box! Note that you can use a beautiful ceramic bowl or any other object as long as it's intended for Reiki. We use a special wooden box that is easy to hold in both hands and is filled at the bottom of the box with crystals. Keep the Healing box in a special place, consider surrounding it with crystals. Try to set aside a set time everyday to send reiki to the people/events etc stored within the healing box. You will find many of the requests for healing stay in there for a few weeks, while some will stay 'forever'. Remember to include your own wishes, worries, any personal development goals you are working on, any physical issues you are addressing for yourself, etc. Also, not to be forgotten, are family members and friends who are ill or otherwise challenged in life and who could sure use a Reiki energy boost. Every day or so read through all the cards in the box and send distant Reiki energy to all the people in it, all at once, to help them heal. As you hear back from people with their healing progress, and using your own intuition, remove some of the cards once reiki has completed its work.

Crystal grid: You charge the crystals with Reiki energy and place them in a set pattern and with a specific intention. Crystals are used to enhance the energy sent at a distance.

Boards with photos and names of people to be healed: Use a bulletin board or any other type of surface where you can attach the names or photos of people requesting Reiki. You can beam the energy to the requests on the board.

Finally, remember to share your distant healing experiences with the recipients if appropriate. Many of your clients could benefit from any insights or intuitive information you may have received from the distant healing session. You can also benefit from any feedback the recipient gives you on the experience. It could help you to fine-tune what you do and the type of technique that works best for you.

As with all things Reiki, the key to success is your Intention.

"Never mistake knowledge for wisdom. One helps you make a living; the other helps you make a life." ~ Sandra Carey

14

Working with Reiki 2

"I must be willing to give up what I am in order to become what I will be." — *Albert Einstein*

Empower Your Goals

Goals make the difference between success and failure in life. Reiki can empower your goals, dreams and desires. Write your goal on a piece of paper. Be specific. A goal should be set in the positive. Include all the facts, dates, names, etc.

For Example: On Monday the 4th July 2011 I John Smith gained entry into Harvard University to study Psychology.

Use Reiki to Help You
Achieve Your Goals

If you have read or watched the movie **The Secret**, you would have heard of the law of attraction. In a nutshell the secret explains that we can have anything we want in life, we just need to send out that thought or vibration to the universe and it will deliver all our goals dreams and desires. By sending out positive energy into the universe, we attract positive results back – It's that simple.

It should also sound very familiar to you as Reiki Practitioners. The Secret or the Law of Attraction is working with the Universal Life Force. You can too; by utilising your Reiki Skills and Knowledge and harnessing the power of Reiki to deliver your wildest dreams and desires.

If you can clearly see in your mind your goals, dreams and desires and you send it out to the universe you will attract everything you desire with the power of Reiki.

Draw the full Reiki sandwich over the top of your goal. Reiki the paper for several minutes; carry the piece of paper with you in your purse or wallet. Reiki the paper several times a day; remember to add the rider should it be for the highest good. Remember – Believe and succeed!

The Magician (Tarot cards)

A simple way of sending Reiki is in the Magician position. Hold one of your hands in the direction you wish to send Reiki and the other pointing down towards the earth.

Preparing To Treat a Client

Clear any negative energy and raise the vibration of the room by using the Cho-Ku-Rei symbol. Draw the CKR symbol on all the walls, ceiling, floor, healing couch, crystals and candles.

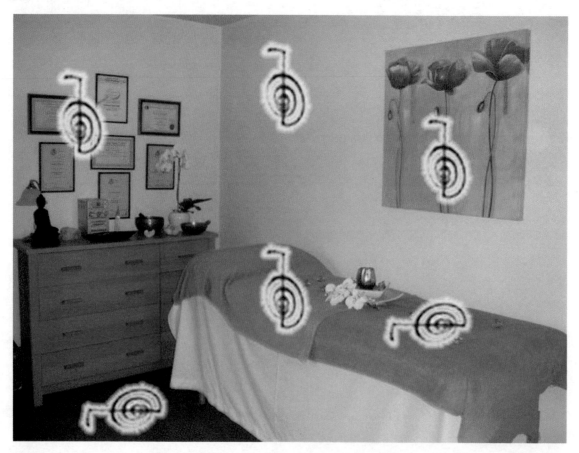

When your client arrives project the CKR symbol onto their third eye chakra to relax and prepare them for a treatment. Always draw the symbols on your hands before you begin the treatment. Visualise the symbols entering your clients' body through each chakra and hand position. Remember to Add the Rider should it be for their Higher Good.

Positive Affirmations

If you are working on a specific treatment try incorporating positive affirmations. For example if your client wants to stop smoking. Ask your client to silently intone at regular intervals throughout the treatment "I now release the need to smoke cigarettes." You should also intone the same affirmation on each new hand position. Pay particular attention to the third eye chakra. Remember the Sei-Heiki is used for addictions.

Alternatively, write the positive affirmation on a piece of paper and have your client hold onto it throughout the treatment. When the treatment is complete your client can take it home with them and keep it in their purse or wallet. Tell them to read it on a regular daily basis.

Scanning the Aura

Before you begin a treatment scan your clients' aura. Use your new heightened intuition to sense possible problems or blockages. Sense how the energy beneath your hands; or in your palms feel. You may notice a variance in temperature. If you are guided or drawn to a particular position on your clients' body go with it. Trust your intuition. Place your hands over that spot and work to heal and re-balance the distortion in your clients' aura.

Zapping

When you use the HSZSN symbol you can zap people or situations from afar. Imagine your hand or finger is a laser gun and beam Reiki where it is needed.

Inspiration usually comes during work, rather than before it. ~ Anon

15

Additional Non Traditional Reiki Symbols

"Those who bring sunshine to the lives of others cannot keep it from themselves." — *J.M. Barrie*

The three traditional Usui symbols cover every eventuality. They are omniscient and omnipotent. However, there are several NON Traditional Reiki symbols which have specific purposes and can be used in conjunction with The Full Reiki Sandwich.

These additional symbols are not an absolute necessity. We believe the student should try using the additional symbols in their daily practice and decide for themselves whether they want to incorporate and use them in their future Reiki Practice.

REVERSED CHO-KU-REI

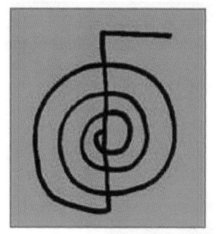 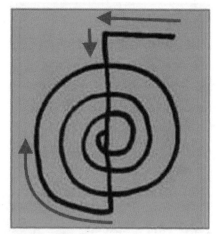

Reversed Cho-Ku_Rei

This symbol is drawn in a clockwise direction unlike the traditional Usui CKR which is drawn anticlockwise. When used together the two CKR's are similar to the double helix found in DNA. The double helix of the DNA is both clockwise and anti-clockwise. The chakras also radiate outwards from the centre of the body similar to the double helix with the narrowest section at the centre.

Full Reiki Sandwich with Reverse CKR

The clockwise CKR connects with heaven while the anti-clockwise CKR connects with earth. You could experiment with both CKR's by using the traditional Usui CKR at the beginning of the Reiki Sandwich and the reversed CKR at the end of the Reiki Sandwich. You may find it brings balance and additional power to your work. If you do notice a positive difference you can incorporate it into your practice and daily use.

ZONAR

Zonar

The Zonar symbol represents infinity, timeless, ageless, perpetual and eternal. It is drawn as the letter Z with the last stroke rising up into the infinity sign drawn three times across the centre of the Z. This symbol is used for past life issues and karmic and inter-dimensional problems that are difficult to define. Often there are problems and issues manifesting in our present life that are leftover remnants from a previous life or lives.

HARTH

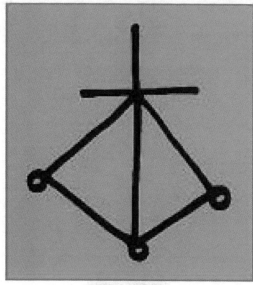

Harth

This is the symbol for love, truth, beauty and harmony. It can be used to dissolve negative patterns we unconsciously use to insulate ourselves from the truth, thus shattering delusion and denial. The Harth Symbol clears and opens the channels to higher consciousness. Often known as the master symbol as it is used in some initiation ceremonies by the Reiki Master. All strokes are from left to right, top to bottom.

How to Draw the Harth Symbol

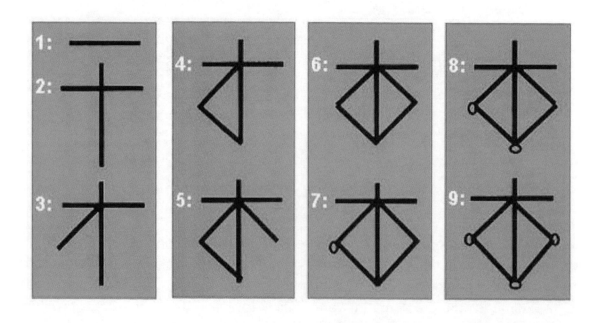

FIRE DRAGON

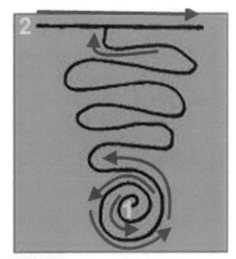

Fire Dragon

Also known as the Tibetan Fire Serpent, this symbol represents the Ki energy travelling up the spine from the root chakra. It is used for spinal and back problems and is said to be good for the menopause. To draw the fire dragon you begin at the base and draw an anti-clockwise spiral two and a half times. Continue the line upwards in a series of waves. Complete the symbol with a horizontal line across the top drawn from left to right. The Fire Dragon's surging upward spiral of energy cleanses and joins the chakra's.

JOHRE

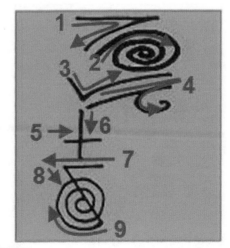

Johre

The Johre symbolises white light. It is used to release blockages, for protection and to transfer healing white light. The symbol can be added to the Reiki Sandwich to send healing energy and protection across space and time. This symbol is difficult to draw so try to project the symbol from your third eye chakra. Draw from top to bottom as shown.

MOTOR ZANON

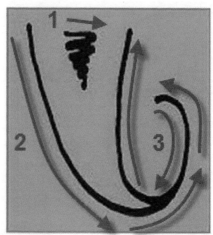

Motor Zanon

Considered a Master symbol by Buddhist monks who use it for exorcism. Motor means to go in while Zanon means to come out. This symbol is used for viruses, infections and Aids. When the motor goes in, the little squiggle catches the virus or bacteria. The Zanon symbol is then drawn and it reverses polarity and leaves the body taking the virus or bacteria with it. Draw the Reiki Sandwich as Follows: 1) CKR 2) Motor Zanon 3) Reverse CKR. (CKR+MZ+RCKR).

REN SO MAI

 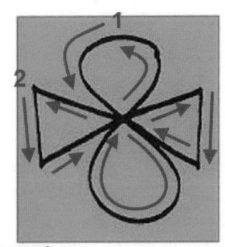

Ren So Mai

Pronounced LEN SO MY this symbol represents pure unconditional love and is used for emotional problems and situations. The symbol is normally placed over the heart chakra.

Draw the figure eight (8) first followed by the dickey-bow shape. Remember to draw from top to bottom, left to right.

RAKU

Raku

This symbol is used for grounding and can be used at the end of each reiki treatment session. Certain Reiki branches use Raku, a Tibetan symbol, to close the connection between teacher and student after attunements. Similar to a lightning stroke, it focuses and grounds (brings into the earth) energy. This symbol is also incorporated into the Tibetan Dai Ko Myo (Tibetan Master symbol) and in an elongated form in the Tibetan Fire Serpent which are taught in the third degree.

OM

OM

OM is a Sanskrit symbol used for protection, healing and meditation and by different Eastern spiritual practices, including yoga. Om represents the sound of the universe and is frequently chanted. It sounds like "ah-oh-mm" or "aum." Some Reiki branches, including Karuna Reiki, use this symbol. Listening to or chanting the sound "om" helps to connect spiritually. Some Reiki masters play om chanting music during the attunement process, or during a healing session.

REMINDER: Always use the Cho-Ku-Rei symbol to activate all of the other symbols and Always intone the name of the each symbol that you have drawn; visualised, or projected it onto a subject, three times.

The most important thing in life is to learn how to give out love,
and to let it come in. ~ Morrie Schwartz

16

Extra Reiki Hand Positions

"What's meant to be will always find a way" — *Trisha Yearwood*

Hand Positions for Treating Specific Parts of the Body

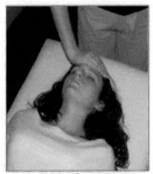

Forehead

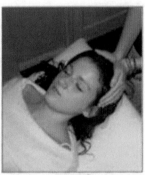

Head

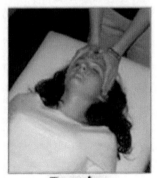

Temples

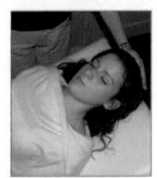

Top of Head

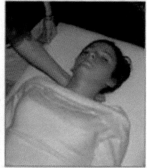

Back of Neck

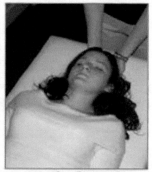

Back of Head

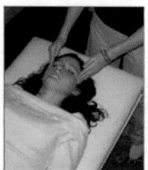

Between Eyes & Temples

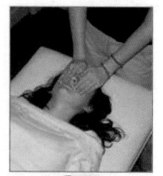

Eyes

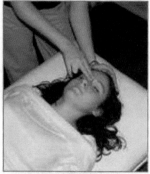

Nasal Bone

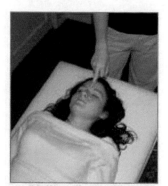

Middle of Forehead

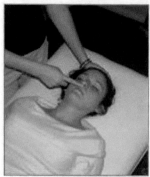

Upper Gum & Mouth

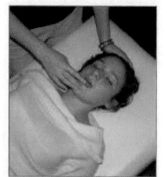

Tongue

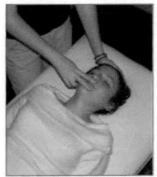

Gums & Mouth

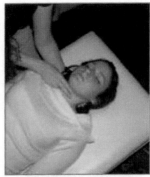

Throat Cartilage

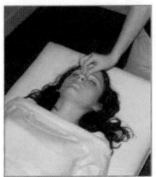

Side of Nose

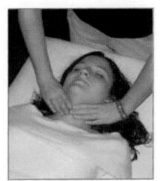

Throat

Breasts

Lungs

Below the sternum

Thymus

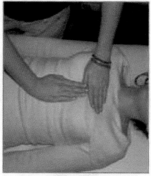

Heart

Liver

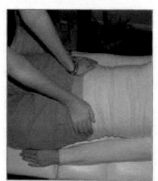

Intestines

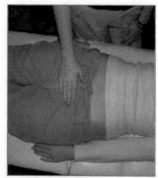

Uterus

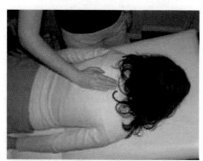

The Spine

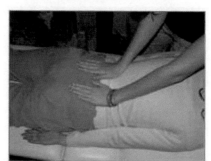

Lumbar Vertebrae 1-5

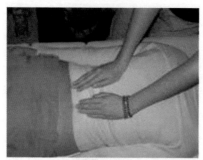

Kidneys

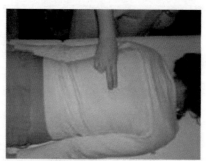

Vertebrae 4-5

Hand Positions for Treating Everyday Complaints

While full body treatments are ideal, some positions are helpful with certain specific conditions or symptoms.

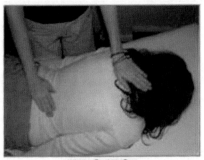

Back Pain

Colds and Flu

Constipation

Coughs

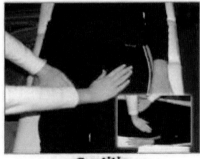

Cystitis

Diarrhoea

Ear Infections

Fever

Flatulence

Food Intolerance

Fungal Infection

Haemorrhoids

Headache

Indigestion

Insomnia

Jet Lag

Knee Problems

Leg Cramps

Mouth Ulcers

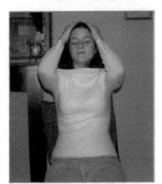

Panic Attacks

PMS

Sinusitis

Swollen Glands

Tonsillitis

Toothache

Viral Infections

Hand Positions for Treating Chronic Complaints

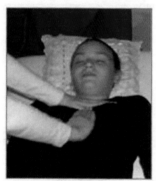

Angina

Arthritis

Asthma

Blood Pressure

Bronchitis

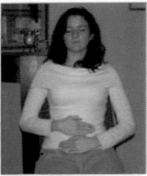

Cancer

Cholesterol

DVT

Depression

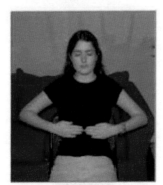

Eczema

Glandular Fever

Hay Fever

HIV (Aids)

IBS

Migraine

RSI

Rheumatism

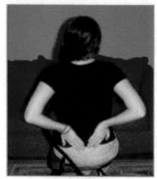

Sciatica

Excellence is not a singular act, but a habit.
You are what you repeatedly do ~ Shaquille O'Neal

17

Combining Reiki with other Healing Disciplines

"The flower that blooms in adversity is the rarest and most beautiful of all." — Walt Disney Company, Mulan

Reiki can complement and enhance the effectiveness of almost any other method of healing you may currently be working with or may work with in the future. Reiki energy balances the subtle frequencies of the person's energetic body as it is being received. So it can be combined with any other therapy to achieve deeper and more profound healing. In Fact, Combining Healing Modalities can help to increase the benefits of a Reiki healing session for the recipient.

As Clinical Hypnotherapists and Master Practitioners of NLP we have found combining Reiki with NLP and Hypnosis can help to really enhance a client session by allowing the client to relax deeply and easily with Reiki, so they are open to at an unconscious level to the positive suggestions of change delivered with NLP and Hypnosis.

Remember if you are going to combine healing modalities you must first explain to your client what you intend to do during the session and get permission from them to use more than just Reiki. You could of course just use Reiki and remain with the viewpoint that Reiki will go where it is needed and do what is needed to facilitate change and healing.

We have found that when for instance a client wants to quit smoking, Reiki and hypnotic suggestion can be quicker and more effective. Below are a couple of examples of how you can combine Reiki with other healing modalities, but remember you are only limited by your imagination.

Reiki and the Art of Focusing

Most people today are aware of the direct connection between the body and mind as it relates to health and well-being. We all store feelings and emotions over our entire lifetime in our bodies. When these feelings and emotions are left to fester they can invariably lead to unhappiness, sickness and disease. The bodymind has an early warning system designed to protect us from impending harm and danger. The signs normally express themselves as bodily aches and pains.

Instead of listening to the body's early warning system which is trying desperately to communicate most people take a pain killer to alleviate and suppress the ailment. Issues, emotions and feelings that need to be dealt with are lock away to cause physical and emotional damage. The body mind and spirit is thrown into state of imbalance. The cure for the pain is in the pain. Through the art of focusing we can communicate with the bodymind and release the blockages and destructive emotions.

Health, well-being and balance follows. Learning to communicate and understand your bodymind is vitally important in the search for longevity and happiness.

The Focusing Technique for Self Healing

Sit or lie down in a comfortable position. Close your eyes. Focus on your breathing. Begin a normal Reiki self healing treatment. Work from position 1 (as illustrated in lesson eight in the first degree home study course) through to position 7. When you have finished working on the heart chakra (position 7) rest both hands across your chest covering your heart.

Focus your conscious awareness inside. Imaging placing a microscopic version of yourself underneath your hands. Feel how safe and relaxed you feel. Allow the miniature version of yourself to travel all over your body from the tips of your toes to the top of your head. Notice any aches or pains that have appeared. If nothing appears straight away look again. Often you will find an ache or pain on the second or third run.

Place your full awareness into the pain. Focus and stay with it for a few moments. Say hello to the pain. Thank the part of the body that has come to talk to you today. Notice what colour it is? (e. g, red). Notice what shape it has? (e.g., square). If that part could communicate with you and could say only one word what would it be? (e.g., sad).

Focus on the word sad (or any other word that comes up). Ask the word sad when it first entered your body. You will normally invoke a memory. Warning you may get tearful and emotional. You may want to cry, shout or scream — let it out.

Continue the conversation with the part of the body until you have resolved the problem, emotion or issue. Use Reiki to heal. If you find it is too difficult to talk and continue the conversation send Reiki to the situation so it can heal it for you with its infinite wisdom. Complete session with the full self treatment.

On occasions you may find these issues are residues left over from past lives, childhood and times of personal loss and grieving. Use the full Reiki Sandwich to heal and remove the emotional and physical pain. This is an extremely powerful technique. Go carefully in the beginning until you have gain confidence and experience with it. If you find it too difficult to work directly with your various issues write them down on a piece of paper and send Reiki to them.

As you release the emotional blockages and residues you will feel a new sense of peace and well-being. Remember to heal yourself first, then your family, then your friends and others.

This technique can be adapted and used to treat others also.

Timeline Reiki

This technique is based on a mixture of Reiki and NLP (neuro linguistic programming). It allows you to travel into your future and create the life you want for yourself.

Sit or lie down in a comfortable position. Close your eyes. Focus on your breathing. Begin a normal Reiki self healing treatment. Work from position 1 through to position 7. When you have finished working on the heart chakra (position 7) rest both hands across your chest covering your heart.

Focus your conscious awareness upwards towards the crown chakra. Visualise or imagine a small opening appear in the crown chakra. Float upwards through the opening and hover just above your body. (You may find you need to open your eyes to visualise or imagine.) Look down and visualise or imagine your timeline. Typically you will see a line of images relating to past memories and future expectations. Normally the future projects forward while the past extends behind you. Whatever is right for you will appear.

Float gently above your timeline. Move forward until you reach the end of your timeline. If your timeline has ended before you can see that you have reached an old age or achieved your full potential project the Full Reiki Sandwich onto your timeline. Take hold of your timeline and stretch it out to add longevity, well-being and a rich fulfilling future.

Look back now along your timeline and review your life. See if you are satisfied with how you have lead your life. Did you reach your full potential? Did you make a worthwhile contribution to this world? Are you satisfied you lived your life to the full? Would you like to change anything about your life? If you find a part (or parts) of your future timeline you want to change project the Full Reiki Sandwich onto that part (or parts). Visualise or imagine the infinite wisdom of Reiki dissolving the unwanted part of your future and replacing it with a new more positive, enriching and fulfilling part.

Look back along your timeline again and feel, sense, imagine, visualise a happier more fulfilling future. Envelop your timeline in the healing guiding light of Reiki. Now look back at the wise old person you will become. Notice the future you has a gift for you. It may be words of wisdom or something that is very important to you on a personal level. Take your gift and give thanks to your future self for this wonderful present. Take a moment to assimilate and really appreciate this wonderful gift you have received.

Gently float back along your timeline to the present you reviewing your new future timeline along the way until you come to a stop above yourself in the present time. Look back into your past, see a younger you who once anticipated the present you. Send Reiki back with its infinite wisdom. Then look into your future and see the future you who is expecting you. Send Reiki into the future.

Gently float back down through the opening in your crown chakra. Bring your awareness and your gift back down to your heart chakra beneath your hands. Place the gift you received from your future wise self into your heart chakra. Feel, sense, experience the new you. Use this gift wisely. Allow the process of Tranceformation and change to begin. Complete the Reiki treatment by finishing all the self healing hand positions. At your own time and pace gently open your eyes.

Timeline Reiki can be adapted to be used with other people.

Limitations live only in our minds. But if we use our imaginations, our possibilities become limitless. ~ Jamie Paolinetti

Congratulations on Completing Your Study of Reiki Level 2

We would like to congratulate you on completing the **Essence of Reiki 2** – our manual which we use in our Certified Usui Advanced Reiki Practitioner workshops and Home Study Courses.

We are both honoured and blessed that we have been able to guide you along this spiritual path to a new future filled with the power, beauty and wonder of Reiki. We hope you will embrace Reiki into your life and allow it to envelope and inspire you in your future.

Love and Light

Garry & Adele Malone

Reiki Master/Teachers Since 1997

If you would like more information about our Certified Usui Reiki Home Study courses please visit http://reiki-store.co.uk to discover how you can become a Certified Usui Reiki Master Teacher.

If you would like more information about our Reiki Practice Development Home Study courses please visit http://reiki-store.com and discover how we can help mentor and guide you build a thriving reiki practice.

Made in the USA
Lexington, KY
01 April 2016